Prison-ese
A Survivor's Guide to Speaking Prison Slang

by Gary K. Farlow, J.D.

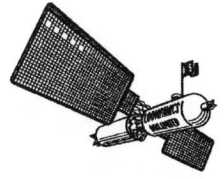

**Loompanics Unlimited
Port Townsend, Washington**

Neither the author nor the publisher assumes any responsibility for the use or misuse of information contained in this book. It is sold for entertainment purposes only. Be warned!

Prison-ese
A Survivor's Guide to Speaking Prison Slang
© 2002 by Gary K. Farlow, J.D.

All rights reserved. No part of this book may be reproduced or stored in any form whatsoever without the prior written consent of the publisher. Reviews may quote brief passages without the written consent of the publisher as long as proper credit is given.

Published by:
Loompanics Unlimited
PO Box 1197
Port Townsend, WA 98368

Loompanics Unlimited is a division of Loompanics Enterprises, Inc.
Phone: 360-385-2230
Fax: 360-385-7785
E-mail: service@loompanics.com
Web site: www.loompanics.com

Cover by R.L. Crabb

ISBN 1-55950-228-2
Library of Congress Card Catalog Number 2002103994

Notes

Although years have elapsed since **Prison-ese** was first written in 1997, very little has actually changed in the prison environment other than the continued growing population. The terms contained in this dictionary are as applicable in 2002 as they were in 1997 when first committed to paper.

Prison-ese has given a large segment of the non-incarcerated population a true insight into the prison subculture. It is with this interest in mind that I have updated **Prison-ese**. The population of our nation's prisons is now approaching two million. When **Prison-ese** was first written, it was just a little over 1.3 million. The alarming increase in the number of people incarcerated gives even more reason for our society to find alternatives to a system that has failed. With a recidivism rate of nearly 85%, the amount of money being used to subsidize an already overburdened system simply no longer makes any sense. Many inmates will tell you that for them, prison is a vacation from obligations: to family, to creditors, to life. This does not imply that serving time in the United States is easy. Far from it. It does imply that the use of prison as a deterrent to crime no longer works in American society. It is a noble experiment that has failed.

It would be unfair not to point out the thousands of corrections staff who *do* attempt to help men and women in the system change their lives. I have met many of these fine, professional persons who truly endeavor to make a difference in a world that is brutal, cynical and self-serving. However, for every one member of the correctional staff that truly does try, there exist at least five who do not and are merely on their job for a paycheck or to "grind an axe" over unresolved issues in their own lives. Many are victims of crime; some are relatives of victims.

Prison-ese illustrates the harsh and vulgar world behind the concrete and barbed-wire of American prisons. It has been said that a society's level of civilization can be judged by the manner in which it treats its incarcerated. If such is the case, then today's penal system is an indictment of our entire criminal justice process, and especially of the correctional system left largely unchecked in the United States today.

Gary K. Farlow

Introduction

"If you loan me your car, I'll put some gas in it." This statement sounds like a teenager attempting to borrow a father's car for a Saturday night date. In prison, this statement means, "If you'll loan me your radio, I'll put some new batteries in it." "Prison-ese" is fast becoming a new dialect of the vast and growing subculture in our nation's prisons and correctional facilities. With nearly two million people currently incarcerated in the United States, this guide to prison slang was developed to be a useful tool for staff, volunteers, family members, and of course, the inmates themselves.

All of the terms and phrases in this "dictionary" were collected by the author over a period of ten years while incarcerated in the North Carolina Department of Corrections, Division of Prisons. Attempts have been made to define each term as accurately as possible. Included along with each definition is an example of how the term might be used in a sentence, in an effort to add clarity to the word's meaning and demonstrate its common usage. It should be noted that many of the words and phrases are explicit, vulgar and graphic.

Prison-ese
A Survivor's Guide
To Speaking Prison Slang

In addition to being a useful guide for the understanding of terminology, **Prison-ese** offers insight into the criminal mind and the subculture of our nation's penal system. Many of the terms are suggestive of the attitudes toward incarceration, the prison system, correctional staff, women and many other social issues. This book can be a useful tool for correctional staff, but also offers valuable information for the sociologist, cultural anthropologist, and for the field of psychology. For example, the number of terms or phrases used to refer to a specific phenomenon is suggestive of that term's importance within the prison culture.

It is hoped that **Prison-ese** proves to be an educational, informative and useful tool to the reader. Currently, this volume is being used at both Anson Community College and Guilford Technical Community College in North Carolina as a resource in their respective Criminal Justice degree programs. It is the author's request that the user/reader please notify the author of any errors, additions and needed changes.

Gary K. Farlow, J.D.

Alphabetical Listing

Aa

AC/DC: To take turns in homosexual activity. Usually refers to one partner inserting his penis into the other partner's anus, then allowing the other partner to insert his penis into his rectum. For example, "Tim and Drew are into that AC/DC thing." Also, see "catcher," "flip flop," "pancake," "pitcher," and "swap out."

Bb

baby life: A life prison sentence of which the offender must serve a minimum of ten years before being considered for release from prison. For example, "Alvin has a baby life."

Prison-ese
A Survivor's Guide
To Speaking Prison Slang

baby raper: A term used to identify an inmate who is serving a sentence for child molestation. For example, "That dude is a baby raper." Also, see "Chester," "chicken hawk."

back biter: One who is devious. One who surprises someone. One who tricks someone. One who lies to someone. One who tells someone one thing and then does another. One who does harmful things to a person while pretending to be their friend. For example, "I thought that Tom was my friend, but he turned out to be a back biter."

bad news: A reference with negative connotations, to someone with a bad reputation. A reference to someone who is no good, a liar, a "snitch," and does not pay their debts. For example, "Robert won't pay you back. He's bad news."

bagged and tagged: To be counted by a D.O.C. correctional officer at count times. For example, "It's count time, time to get bagged and tagged."

ball: Money, in the amount of one dollar. For example, "Say, homeboy, can you loan me a ball?" Also, see "blade," and "rock."

balloon: To put something into a balloon, usually illegal drugs, and swallow it, with the intention of retrieving it from the feces after a bowel movement. For example, "He used a balloon to get cocaine into the prison."

beat down: To overcome. To out do. To humiliate or gain the upper hand. To add insult to injury. For example, "The parole board won't let me go. They just keep on beating me down." "I played cards with him and I beat him down."

beat it: To leave or request someone else to leave. For example, "I ain't giving you a dime, so beat it."

beat your feet: An impolite request or demand for another person to leave. For example, "Hey, man, I ain't got nothing to say to you, so why don't you beat your feet?" Also, see "beat it," "burn the road up," "let your clutch out," and "pop your clutch."

beat your meat: A reference to masturbation. For example, "You're lying if you say you don't beat your meat." "Doug was in the bathroom beating his meat."

been down: A phrase referring to serving time in prison. For example, "I been down for nine years." Also, see "chain gang," and "doing time."

big house: A dated expression to refer to prison. For example, "I been in the big house all my life." "I wrote my folks and told them I'm in the big house now."

bitch: 1. A female. For example, "She's a good looking bitch." 2. A conviction for an habitual felon. An abbreviation for "habitual." For example,

Prison-ese
A Survivor's Guide
To Speaking Prison Slang

"I got the bitch for grand larceny." Also, see "the bitch."

bitchin': 1. Complaining. For example, "He was bitchin' about his sentence." 2. Exceptionally good or nice. For example, "That's a bitchin' pair of shoes."

blade: One dollar. A "ball." Also referred to as a "rock." For example, "I need a blade."

blank: To lose self-control. To use poor judgment. To behave in a bizarre or unusual manner. To become angry. To go into a rage. For example, "I asked Phillip a question and he blanked on me and started acting like he wanted to fight."

blasé blasé: Et cetera, et cetera. And other things of the same class; and so forth. A number of unspecified things or persons. A miscellany of extras. Additional odds and ends. For example, "The parole board told me I needed a home plan, a job plan, blasé blasé."

blind side: To take someone by surprise. To catch by surprise. For example, "I didn't see it coming. He blind sided me."

blood: An African-American person. A person of African-American heritage. A black person. For example, "He's a blood." Also, see "brother."

bloodman: Dreadlock expression for a person with a reputation as a troublemaker. A misfit. For example, "Stay away from that guy. He's a bloodman."

blow: 1. To sing, particularly when the singing is good. For example, "Janet Jackson can really blow." 2. To be angry. To rage. For example, "I wouldn't push him too hard. He'll blow." Also, see "blank" and "go off."

blunt: Marijuana rolled up in cigar tobacco. For example, "Hey, man, let's roll a blunt."

blunted: To be high or stoned by smoking a blunt. For example, "John's blunted."

bo-bos: Canvas shoes, of poor quality, issued by the Department of Corrections. They are avoided by inmates if at all possible. For example, "I know he ain't got no money. He wears them bo-bos."

boche boy: A dreadlock expression for someone who is homosexual. For example, "Hey, mon, he's a boche boy."

boo: A girlfriend or boyfriend. A lover or sweetheart. A significant other. For example, "My boo's coming up to see me on Sunday."

boomerang: A recidivist. A repeat offender. Someone who has served multiple prison sentences. For example, "Jeff is a boomerang."

Prison-ese
A Survivor's Guide
To Speaking Prison Slang

boost: To encourage someone to do something. To encourage or promote. To agitate. To facilitate. To incite. For example, "Jack was trying to boost Dan into fighting with Bill, but Dan didn't go for it."

bossman: A term used to refer to anyone with power or authority. It is also used as a general greeting in reference to both inmates and staff. Depending on its usage, it can have either a positive or negative connotation. For example, "Hey, bossman, can I get a phone call?" (Usage toward a staff member.) "Yo, bossman, can you get me a soda from the canteen?" (Usage toward an inmate.)

boulder baby: Someone who uses or is addicted to rock cocaine. For example, "He spends all his money on that rock. He ain't nothin' but a boulder baby."

boy: A prison inmate who engages in homosexual activity; usually dominated by a more aggressive inmate under terms of duress, for protection or because the weaker inmate is in debt. For example, "Tim is John's boy." Also, see "canteen baby," "daddy," and "state daddy."

break his grill: To hit someone in the teeth, mouth or face. For example, "I'm going to break his grill."

break me off a little something: 1. To request something from another person. For example, "Hey, Mike, break me off a little something." 2. To threaten with physical harm. For example, "If you don't get me my money, I might have to break me off a little something."

break off something in you: 1. To threaten another with sexual violence. To imply anal intercourse. 2. To make a threat of physical harm. To imply the use of a shank or knife. For example, "I'm going to break something off in you." "Pay up today or I'm going to break something off in you."

brother: An African-American person. Afro-American. A person of African-American heritage. A black person. For example, "He's a brother." Also, see "blood."

browned down: To be demoted from minimum custody to medium or close custody. For example, "Rick was browned down."

buck: Homemade wine; something made with dried fruit and/or yeast. For example, "The guys in the dorm are making buck." See also, "hooch," and "mash."

bug: A term used to refer to someone who suffers from a mental health condition or mental illness. A person who exhibits strange or peculiar behavior. For example, "That guy is really a bug." A synonymous expression is "bug case."

bug doctor: A term used to refer to any mental health professional; a psychiatrist, psychologist,

Prison-ese
A Survivor's Guide
To Speaking Prison Slang

behavioral specialist, social worker, etc. For example, "Bob was called up to see the bug doctor today."

bug juice: Psychotropic medication. Medications which affect the central nervous system. Medications prescribed by a psychiatrist. For example, "Andy takes that bug juice for his nerves."

bug out: To behave in a bizarre or unusual manner. To exhibit behavior suggestive of poor judgment or mental illness. For example, "Steve, you're not going to bug out on me, are you?"

bug unit: Term used to identify a housing unit which is designated for residential mental health inmates.

bumpin': A term used to describe anything which is exceptionally good. For example, "That chocolate cake was really bumpin'."

bumpin' pocket books: A term used to refer to two homosexuals having a relationship; usually used to imply two effeminate or "queen" gays having a relationship. For example, "Man, look at them two queens bumpin' pocket books."

bunk: Place where one inmate sleeps. Bed. For example, "I'm tired. I think I'll go lay on my bunk for awhile." Also, see "rack."

Alphabetical Listing

9

burn it up: A reference to having used all the money in one's trust fund. For example, "Man, that Shawn just got in some money and he's already burnt it up."

burn one: A reference to smoking a cigarette. To smoke a cigarette or a cigar. To smoke marijuana. A request for a cigarette or marijuana. To take a break to smoke. For example, "Hey, Lance, let's go burn one."

burn the road up: To leave the area. To be told to leave another's presence. For example, "The officer told everyone to burn the road up." Also, see "Don't let the door hit you where the Lord split you," "Let me see the back of your head get small," "Let the clutch out," and "Pop your clutch."

bust a grape: A phrase often issued as a challenge for someone to take some action. A dare. An insult. To call another's bluff. For example, "You ain't gonna do nuthin'. You wouldn't bust a grape." "He ain't gonna bust a grape."

bust your head: To fight. To assault another. For example, "You better burn the road up or I'm gonna bust your head."

**Prison-ese
A Survivor's Guide
To Speaking Prison Slang**

Cc

cadillac: 1. Any name brand cigarette, as opposed to an economy brand or hand-rolled cigarette. For example, "John's got it going on, man. He smokes them cadillacs." 2. A term frequently used to refer to something nice, such as a radio. For example, "Say, Brian, that's a bitchin' Cadillac you got there."

can: Toilet. Restroom. Bathroom. For example, "Charles went to the can."

canteen baby: An inmate who has a reputation for relying on others to buy items for him from the canteen or inmate commissary. An inmate who performs sexual acts for canteen items. For example, "That Tony ain't nothin' but a canteen baby."

car: A radio. For example, "I got to borrow somebody's car."

Alphabetical Listing

11

carbon monoxide high: To travel by motor vehicle, typically a prison transfer bus. Also used when expressing a desire to leave a prison unit or transfer to another. For example, "I need a carbon monoxide high." Also, see "smell some gas."

carry it to the door: A reference to having served all of one's prison sentence. For example, "Man, that Jimmy is going to carry it to the door." Also, see "max out."

carry yourself: Demeanor. Personality. Outward appearance. For example, "People in prison judge a guy by the way he carries himself."

catcher: A reference to the receptive partner in a male homosexual act. Refers to the sexual partner who has the other partner's penis inserted into his mouth or anus. For example, "I saw Bobby puttin' the meat to Ryan. Ryan was playing catcher."

chain gang: An antiquated term referring to working on a road crew or road squad when inmates used to wear leg irons and were chained together. In current use, this term is loosely used to refer to being incarcerated. To be locked up. To be in prison. For example, "I've been on the chain gang for five years now." Also, see "been down," and "doing time."

check-off: A term with strongly negative connotations, used to refer to an inmate who has re-

Prison-ese
A Survivor's Guide
To Speaking Prison Slang

quested protective custody to avoid being harmed by another inmate. An inmate may also check-off indirectly by getting a write-up and going to segregation to avoid trouble, being harmed, to avoid paying a debt, etc. The act of seeking protective custody or going to segregation to avoid any negative consequences. For example, "William is a check-off." "Jerry checked-off to avoid having to pay back the loan sharks." "Richard went to check-off when he found out he had a contract out on him for not paying his gambling debts." Also, see "honeycomb hide out."

Chester: A term used to refer to an inmate serving a sentence for child molestation. For example, "I heard that John is a Chester."

chicken hawk: A man who prefers adolescents as sexual partners. An inmate who prefers young male inmates as sexual partners. For example, "James talks about all the girls, but he's really just a chicken hawk." Also, see "do the boys."

chicken scratch: A small sum of money. For example, "That ain't going to cost you a dime. It's just chicken scratch." Also, see "chump change."

chill: To calm down. To avoid unusual behavior. To avoid behavior which would attract attention. Also, "chill out," "take a chill pill." For example, "Chill, man, here comes the C.O."

Alphabetical Listing

chokin' the chicken: A reference to male masturbation. For example, "John is in the shower again chokin' the chicken."

chow: Food. A meal. For example, "Let's go get some chow."

chow down: To eat. To eat rapidly. To have a meal. For example, "Hey, dude, let's go chow down."

chow hall: Inmate cafeteria. The building where food is served in the prison. For example, "It's about time to go to the chow hall for lunch." Also, see "ptomaine domain."

chronic: Strong, potent or powerful marijuana. For example, "His boy has that chronic."

chump change: A dated term used to describe a small sum of money. For example, "Hey, Ron, that's just chump change." Also, see "Chicken scratch."

click: To have money deposited into one's inmate trust fund. This term is especially heard on prison units that use the inmate ID cards instead of issuing cash. For example, "Hey, man, are you gonna click on Friday?"

clockin': A reference to making a lot of money. For example, "Bob is really clockin'."

Prison-ese
A Survivor's Guide
To Speaking Prison Slang

closet queen: A secretive homosexual. For example, "Johnny doesn't want anybody to know he's gay. He's just a closet queen."

coal burner: A white inmate who engages in homosexual acts with a black inmate. For example, "Tom is a coal burner."

C.O.: Term used for a correctional officer. For example, "Hey, C.O., come unlock the gate."

cock: A term used to refer to both the penis and vagina. For example, "He was jacking his cock." "When I get out, first thing I'm gonna do is find me some cock."

cock diesel: Very strong. Very powerful. For example, "Sam can bench press over 500 pounds. He's cock diesel." Also, see "diesel."

Colonel Klink: A reference to any correctional officer of rank above a sergeant. For example, "Hell, here comes Colonel Klink." Also, see "white shirt."

come get you: A challenge to fight. A challenge to correct an alleged wrong by fighting. A suggestion to an adversary that he will have to use physical force if he wishes to get revenge or bring about change. For example, "If you don't like it, then come get you." Also, see "my mouth ain't bleeding."

contract: An agreement. More frequently used to refer to a bounty offered for the recovery of property or money and/or to injure or kill another inmate. For example, "Yo, man, I thought we had a contract." "Al checked-off when he heard that there was a contract out on him."

convict: A dated term, but used today to refer to an inmate who has served a considerable amount of time or who has been in prison before. Also used to distinguish an inmate from those considered untrustworthy. For example, "Man, I can't stand all these inmates. I'm from the old school when it was just us convicts." "You can trust Tom. He's a convict."

cracker: A racial slur, referring to a white person. Also used to identify a redneck. For example, "That dude's just a cracker."

crib: Street language for a bed or a home. An apartment. A dormitory. Where one sleeps. For example, "I'll catch you later. I'm going back to the crib."

cruisin': Aimlessly walking. This term can also mean looking for sexual contact. For example, "I'm not going anywhere in particular. I'm just cruisin'."

cut: Any reference to serving less than the maximum of one's prison sentence. For example, "Gary went back to court to try to get a time cut."

**Prison-ese
A Survivor's Guide
To Speaking Prison Slang**

"I got 14 cut to 7." (A reference to serving half of a 14-year sentence under the Fair Sentencing Act.)

cut me some slack: A rather dated term, used to imply needing some room or space. To give a break. To receive less than the maximum penalty. To show mercy. To receive a suspended sentence. To make allowances. For example, "They cut me some slack and let me out of the hole early."

Dd

daddy: The dominant partner of two men who engage in homosexual activity in prison. For example, "That's John's daddy." Also, see "state daddy."

DAP: A modified handshake. A greeting. Hitting fists together. For example, "Yo, homeboy, give me some DAP."

diesel: Strong. Powerful. For example, "For his size, he can bench press a lot. He's diesel." Also, see "cock diesel."

Alphabetical Listing

dip my wick: To have sexual intercourse. For example, "Johnny wants to dip his wick in something."

dissed: A term used to refer to showing disrespect. For example, "We was all dissing the officer."

dl (down low): A term referring to discretion. To do something discreetly. For example, "On the dl, I know where the mojo is."

do the boys: To participate in homosexual activity. For example, "Terry doesn't do the boys." Also, see "chicken hawk."

doc: A term used to refer to any medical staff member, i.e., medical doctor, nurse, social worker, psychologist, rehabilitation therapist, dentist, dental assistant, optometrist, behavioral specialist, psychiatrist, correctional health assistant, etc. For example, "I've got a bad cold. I guess I better sign up to see the doc."

dog: 1. A dated term used to refer to an unattractive female. For example, "I don't know what he sees in her, she's a dog, a real bow wow." Also, see "mud duck," and "skeezer." 2. To harass. To be persistent. Relentless. To take advantage of. For example, "Don't dog me. I said I'd pay you back when I get the money."

dog boy: A term referring to an inmate whose job it is to take care of the prison dogs, usually blood-

Prison-ese
A Survivor's Guide
To Speaking Prison Slang

hounds, which are used to track escapees. For example, "Billy was the dog boy before he transferred here."

doggin' me: Harass. To take advantage of. To pester. To bother. For example, "He's been doggin' me for two weeks to do that legal work for him."

doing good: To have some money. For example, "Webster is doing good." Also, see, "living large."

don't be the one: A threat. For example, "Don't be the one to give me a lifer for killing you." Also, see "Don't let today be the day," and "Don't make it happen."

don't let today be the day: A threat. For example, "Don't let today be the day you die and I go to the chair." Also, see "Don't be the one," and "Don't make it happen."

don't make it happen: A threat. For example, "Look, I warned you once already, don't make it happen." Also, see "Don't be the one" and "Don't let today be the day."

double bagger: 1. A dated term used to identify an unattractive female. 2. A female who is so unattractive that one would need to put two bags over her head when having sexual intercourse with her. 3. A female who is so unattractive that one would need two bags to have sex with her, one bag to put over her head, and another to vomit in if the first bag fell off her head. For example, "She's really ugly, a double bagger."

dove: 1. A five-dollar bill. For example, "He owes me a dove." Also, see "nickel," and "pound." 2. A weak or passive inmate. For example, "Bill is a dove." 3. A term of endearment or acceptance. For example, "Hey, dove, how's my baby doing?"

down: A reference to serving a prison sentence. Serving time. Incarceration. Also, see "been down." For example, "I been down for nearly ten years now."

down like four flat tires: To be the best of friends. To stand by someone. To fully support someone, no matter what. For example, "Me and Jim are down like four flat tires."

downside: A reference to having completed over one-half of one's prison sentence. For example, "I'm on the downside of my time now."

draggin' me: A term referring to the belief that the "system" is personally persecuting the inmate by interfering with his progress through the prison system and his eventual release. For example, "They just keep draggin' me, man." "They won't give me my honor grade. They're just draggin' me."

Prison-ese
A Survivor's Guide
To Speaking Prison Slang

dread: A person who has their hair in locks, braids or dread locks. A Rastafarian. For example, "He's a dread."

dread locks: Braided hair or wearing the hair in locks. Long, thin braids or natural locks of hair densely radiating from the scalp, in a style popularized by the Rastafarians of Jamaica. For example, "He wears dread locks."

drive: To borrow someone's radio. For example, "How about letting me drive for awhile?"

duckin' and dodgin': Avoiding something or someone. Maneuvering to avoid blows in a fight. For example, "Pete was duckin' and dodgin' and getting in a few good punches." "He's been duckin' and dodgin' me for weeks."

face: 1. A term referring to one's reputation or credibility. For example, "He had to straighten his face," meaning he had to take some action to maintain his credibility. 2. A term also yelled out by observers during a basketball game when someone scores a point from the three-point line. For example, "Face."

fell: A term referring to incarceration. The time at which an offender began serving his prison sentence. For example, "I fell in 1985," meaning "I entered prison in 1985."

fight game: A term referring to a person's ability to physically fight. For example, "John doesn't have much of a fight game."

fine: A term referring to a person's physical attractiveness or beauty. It has a positive connotation. For example, "Man, she's fine as hell."

five'o: A police officer or correctional officer. For example, "Hey, guys, chill out. Here comes the five'o." Also, see "the man."

flip: Inconsistent. Flippant. Erratic behavior. Unreliable. To change one's mind often. For example, "She's flip. One week she comes to see me, then the next week she wants a divorce."

flip flop: Used to refer to males who engage in both heterosexual and homosexual behavior. For example, "That Nathan is a flip flop." Also, see "catcher," "pancake," "pitcher," and "swap out."

flip your stick: To move the penis out of the way during a strip search. For example, "I don't like

Prison-ese
A Survivor's Guide
To Speaking Prison Slang

the way you have to flip your stick during the strip search."

freak: Someone who is sexually promiscuous. Excessively sexually active. Someone who is easy to engage in a sexual act. Kinky. A fetishist. For example, "She's easy man, a real freak." "He's wide open, dudes, a freak from jump street."

from the get-go: From the beginning. From the start. For example, "He's been nothin' but trouble from the get-go."

front me: 1. To give someone something, with the understanding that payment will be forthcoming in the future. To give someone credit. To make a loan. For example, "Will you front me five bucks 'til payday?" 2. To allow someone in line in front of you in the chow line, canteen line or clothes house line. For example, "Hey, homeboy, how 'bout frontin' me?"

fuck head: A term of negative connotation meant to imply that another person is stupid, or lacks common sense.

Gg

gak: Gun. Weapon. A pistol. For example, "I pulled my gak on her and told the bitch to cough up some cash."

game face: A term referring to impression management. A false front. Façade. An image one attempts to project. For example, "Jim is an okay dude, but that tough guy image is just a game face."

gangster: 1. A true criminal. Antisocial. Member of a street gang. For example, "He's a real gangster." 2. A rap music artist who specializes in songs about the life on the streets. For example, "Tupac was a real gangster man."

gas: A term used to refer to batteries for a radio. For example, "The gas for my car cost me $1.80, man!"

getback: A term referring to revenge. Also "payback." For example, "You did me wrong. Getback is hell."

get blunted: To get stoned or high on a blunt. To smoke marijuana rolled in cigar tobacco. For example, "Let's get blunted."

get it like Tyson: A suggestion to another person that if they want something they will have to take

Prison-ese
A Survivor's Guide
To Speaking Prison Slang

it by force. For example, "If you want your money back, you'll have to get it like Tyson."

get it with your muscle: A term suggestive to another person that if they want something, they will have to take it by force. Also, see "get it like Tyson."

get me: A term referring to gratification of one's personal needs or desires. To look out for oneself. To have one's way. For example, "Yo, man, can I get me?" Also, see "Let me get me," and "Let me get that."

get on down the floor: 1. To leave the area. To move away from. For example, "The officer told everyone to get on down the floor." 2. To dance. To "boogie." For example, "Man did you see those girls get on down the floor on *Soul Train?*"

get on the board: To play or gamble on a particular sporting event. To place a bet on a team or race car driver in a pool. For example, "Yo, Mark, you gonna get on the board this week?"

get out of my face: An impolite request or demand for another person to leave. For example, "We're through talkin', so get out of my face." Also, see "burn the road up" and "let your clutch out."

get stupid: A reference to getting high. To get stoned. To get drunk. To use drugs and/or alcohol. To act silly or childish. For example, "Hey, man, let's get some rock and get stupid."

getting down: To be engaged in some activity. To do something. For example, "Everybody was getting down."

go for anything: Gullible. Naïve. To be easily tricked. To be easily manipulated. For example, "Don will go for anything."

go for it: A challenge for someone to do something. To boost. A phrase used to encourage someone to ignore the consequences and go ahead and do something. To proceed without caution or reservation. For example, "I think you ought to go for it." "Go for it!"

go off: To lose self-control. To use poor judgment. To behave in a bizarre or unusual manner. To become angry or go into a rage. For example, "I asked Ray a question and he wanted to go off on me and start a fight." Also, see "blank."

go to his ass: To fight. To threaten bodily harm to someone. To assault someone. For example, "If he lays one hand on me. I'm gonna go to his ass." Also, see "go to war."

go to war: To fight. For example, "If you don't leave me alone man, me and you are going to go to war." Also, see "go to his ass."

Prison-ese
A Survivor's Guide
To Speaking Prison Slang

got it going on: A phrase, with a positive connotation, referring to one who appears competent in many areas. Stability. To have things going in one's favor. For example, "That Kenny's really got it going on."

got it like the Feds got handcuffs: A phrase referring to having a lot of something. An analogy to the FBI having a lot of handcuffs. To have a seemingly endless amount of something. For example, "Webster's got plenty of money. He's got it like the Feds got handcuffs."

got you covered: 1. To protect someone. To look out for someone. To prevent someone from being ambushed or taken by surprise. To watch out for someone. For example, "Don't worry about that threat. I got you covered." 2. To pay someone else's debts. To buy something for someone. To do something for someone. For example, "Hey, I told you to forget about that debt. I got you covered." Also, see "got your back."

got your back: To protect someone. To look out for someone during hard times. To prevent someone from getting hurt or taken by ambush. For example, "Go ahead and take care of business. I got your back." Also, see "got you covered."

greened up: To be promoted to honor grade status or minimum custody. The opposite of "browned down." For example, "They told me today that I'm getting greened up."

grill: A term used to refer to a person's face. Also sometimes used to refer to the teeth or mouth. For example, "He got his grill tore up!"

gun camp: A prison unit where the perimeter is guarded by armed officers. For example, "I was on a gun camp before I got here." Also, see "under the gun."

gunnin' down: A term used to refer to male masturbation while looking at another person, usually a female officer. Voyeurism. For example, "They say John got caught on third shift gunnin' down the C.O."

gunslinger: A term used to identify someone who masturbates frequently. Used to refer to someone who "guns down" the female officers while masturbating. For example, "That guy is a real gunslinger from hell." Also, see "gunnin' down," "pistol Pete," and "shooter."

Hh

hang: To associate with. To persist. For example, "Bill hangs with Pete." Also, see "hang tough," "hang with."

hang tough: To have determination. To refrain from losing hope or giving up. To persist. For example, "I know things are rough, but I got to hang tough."

hang with: To associate with. To have certain individuals as close friends. For example, "He doesn't hang with just anybody." Also, see "hang" and "hang tough."

hawk: 1. To be watchful and alert. To watch closely. To stare. For example, "I had Tim hawk the man for me." Also, see "hawk the man," "sweating." 2. To be an individual who prefers younger sexual partners. To have desires for teenage sexual partners. For example, "That guy is just a hawk." Also, see "baby raper," "Chester," and "chicken hawk."

hawk the man: To be watchful for correctional officers. To be on the look-out for officers while a fellow inmate performs an illegal act. For example, "Hey, hawk the man while I steal me a phone call." Also, see "hawk."

head: 1. Dated term used to refer to the toilet, restroom or bathroom. For example, "Larry had to go to the head." 2. The glans of the penis. The penis. For example, "I put my head up in her."

head doctor: A term used to refer to any mental health professional; a psychiatrist, psychologist, behavioral specialist, social worker, etc. For example, "Bert was called to go see the head doctor." Also, see "bug doctor," and "shrink."

headlights: A reference to a female's breasts. For example, "That chick has a nice set of headlights."

heart: Fortitude. Willingness to stand up for oneself. Assertiveness. Will. Strength. Backbone. To have "heart." For example, "He has heart." Also, see "fight game." The opposite of "having heart" is to "have no heart." Such a term would refer to passivity, lack of assertiveness or being viewed as weak.

he's got sugar in his blood: A phrase referring to being homosexual. For example, "Tom's got sugar in his blood." Also, see "do the boys."

hit: To have sex with. To express a desire to have sex with someone. To make sexual advances toward another person. For example, "I'd like to hit her."

hit the fence: A reference to making an escape from prison. To run and jump on the fence in an effort to climb it and escape from prison. For ex-

Prison-ese
A Survivor's Guide
To Speaking Prison Slang

ample, "Did you hear that Mike hit the fence last night?"

hole: Segregation. Isolation. For example, "I got a write-up and got thrown in the hole for thirty days." Also, see "hole time."

hole time: A term synonymous with "hole." A reference to serving time in segregation, usually for a disciplinary infraction. For example, "Man, I hate doing that hole time."

homeboy: Someone who is from the same hometown as another person. For example, "Joe is Tommy's homeboy." Also, see "homes" and "homie."

homes: A term synonymous with "homeboy." For example, "Hey, homes, how 'bout fronting me a soda 'til payday?"

homie: A term synonymous with "homeboy." For example, "Yeah, he's my homie."

honeycomb hideout: Segregation. Lock up. For example, "That dude owed me money, and he went down to the honeycomb hideout." Differs from "hole" and "hole time," in as much as the phrase honeycomb hideout is used expressly for inmates who request "Protective custody." Also, see "check off" and "P.C."

hooch: Homemade wine; sometimes made with yeast rolls, raisins and/or honey buns from the inmate canteen. For example, "He makes some bumpin' hooch." Also, see "buck" and "mash."

house: A dated term to refer to one's place of residence, but also used in prison to refer to one's dormitory or housing unit. For example, "The man called the yard closed. I better get on back to the house."

hustle: A term used to refer to the manner in which an inmate earns money. For example, "He earns his hustle making them greeting cards."

hype: 1. To make stronger. To strengthen. 2. To make a cigar or cigarette stronger by removing the filter and rerolling the contents. For example, "I like to hype my cigars."

iceman: 1. A term infrequently used to refer to someone who is perceived to be unemotional. One who is cold and aloof. Not easily shaken emotionally. 2. A term used to refer to a killer.

One who is to be avoided for fear of risk of retribution. For example, "Stay away from Tim. That guy's an iceman."

I fell into that: To be tricked. To recognize one's own gullibility. To feel trapped or tricked. For example, "Man, he got my money. I fell into that." Also, see "I went for that."

if you buy, I'll fly: To offer to go get something (typically from the inmate canteen) for someone if they will buy something for you. For example, "Hey, man, if you want a coffee, I'll go get it. If you buy, I'll fly." Also can be used as "If you fly, I'll buy." When the offer is made by the one who is buying.

I got her: To "gun" down someone. To covertly observe another person while having sexual fantasies and masturbating to those fantasies. To masturbate while watching someone, usually a female officer or staff member. Voyeurism. To peep. For example, "Last night, that bitch was working' and I got her." Also, see "gunnin' down," and "I got one."

I got one: To secretly observe someone while masturbating to fantasies of that person. Synonymous with "I got her." For example, "There's three of 'em working, but I got one."

iron pile: A term referring to the area designated for weight lifting. For example, "Meet me at the iron pile after lunch."

it's all good: A phrase which implies, "everything is going to be okay." To mean that it really doesn't matter because everything is still going to turn out alright. For example, "Yo, man, the bitch is divorcing me, but it's all good."

it's dead: A phrase used to express a desire to put an end to an issue. To terminate a discussion of a particular issue. To let the past rest. To allow bygones to be bygones. To indicate that something is over, done with. For example, "Don't sweat it, man. Like I told you, it's dead."

I went for that: Synonymous with "I fell into that." To be tricked. To be fooled. To admit to one's own gullibility. For example, "He sure pulled one over on me and I went for that."

Prison-ese
A Survivor's Guide
To Speaking Prison Slang

Jj

J: 1. A term used to refer to a marijuana cigarette, or joint. For example, "Let me get a hit off that J." 2. In basketball, a dated term which refers to a jump shot. For example, "Hey, man, dig that J he got off."

jack off: To masturbate. Also used as a derogatory remark, which suggests that another person has no worthwhile goals. For example, "Damn, is he in that john again jacking off?" "James is just a jack off."

jailhouse lawyer: A term which refers to an inmate who earns money by assisting others with legal matters, i.e., Motions for Appropriate Relief, appeals and letters to the parole commission. For example, "You need to go see Phil. He's the best jailhouse lawyer on the camp."

jaws: Dated term which refers to the buttocks, usually of a female. "Man, check out the jaws on that chick."

Jody: A man believed to be involved with an inmate's wife. A term for a man who becomes romantically involved with the wife, girlfriend, or lover of a man who is incarcerated. For example, "Ain't no use in crying over her now. Jody done got your woman."

john: Dated expression for the toilet. For example, "Frank went to the john."

Johnson: Penis. For example, "Tim was giving his old Johnson a workout right in front of the bitch."

joint: 1. A dated term, but still widely in use, to refer to a marijuana cigarette. For example, "Barry gots the joints, man. He sells 'em at five bucks each." 2. A dated term used to refer to jail or prison. For example, "I been in this joint for going on ten years."

jones: Thoughts. Feelings. Daydreams. Usually associated with addictive desire for alcohol, drugs, or sex. For example, "He was jonesin' talking about how he used to have all them women."

joog: To tease. To make fun of another person. For example, "I know they are going to joog him when he gets back to the dorm."

jump on you: To fight. To assault someone. For example, "You best burn the road up before I jump on you."

kick it: To talk. To have a conversation. For example, "Come on over, man, and we'll kick it for awhile."

kickin': A reference to something which is exceptional or extremely good. For example, "That fried chicken was kickin'." Also, see "bumpin'."

kick to the curb: To ignore. To abandon. To have nothing more to do with a person after they have been used for whatever purpose the relationship may have been established for. To dump someone when a better offer comes. For example, "I see how it is with you. Now that my money is gone, you just kick me to the curb."

kite: 1. A term used to refer to a message or letter. For example, "My girl sent me a kite today." 2. A term used to refer to the loose tobacco sold in the inmate canteen. For example, "Man, that kite went up to forty-three cents a pack." Also, see "roll-up," and "stud."

kite flush: A method of sending messages by flushing a note down the toilet, with the recipient retrieving the message from the toilet at the other end. Especially used in jails or segregation. This procedure is often accomplished with the use of wire, balloons or string. The term also refers to talking into the toilet, with a recipient listening at another toilet. For example, "Tony sent Jack a kite flush."

knee baby: Next to the youngest child. Second to the last born in a family. For example, "There were seven of us in my family, and I was the knee baby."

knockin' boots: To engage in anal intercourse. Anal sex. For example, "Lance and Don were knockin' boots."

knockin' down: A reference to doing something. Activity. Usually refers to doing something on a large or grand scale, easily or effortlessly. Often used when referring to making a lot of money. For example, "I was knockin' down some bucks out on the street."

knot: A large sum of money. A large roll of paper money. A wad. A wad of money. For example, "Hey, did you see that officer's wallet? He had a knot!"

Ll

leave something for the baby to do: A request for someone to stop whining or complaining. For example, "Shut up, man, and quit yer whining. Leave something for the baby to do."

let me get me: A term used to ask for something, i.e., money, canteen, cigarettes, or food. For example, "Yo, dude, you going to the canteen? Let me get me."

let me get that: 1. Synonymous with "let me get me," and used to ask for something in particular. For example, "That cake looks good. How 'bout let me get that?" 2. A phrase used to imply sexual interest in another person. For example, "She sure is lookin' fine. Let me get that."

let me live: 1. A request that someone stop borrowing or bumming. For example, "Hey, man, quit asking for everything. Let me live." 2. A phrase used by someone who is attempting to borrow or bum something. For example, "Hey, man, you living large. How 'bout let me live?"

let me live with you: A request to bum or borrow from someone else. To ask for money, goods (canteen items), or services. For example, "I saw you got some money in the mail today. How about you let me live with you?"

let me see the back of your head get small: A term used when asking someone to leave. To tell someone to go away. For example, "I'm done talkin'. Now let me see the back of your head get small." Also, see "beat your feet," "burn the road up," "let your clutch out," and "pop your clutch."

let your clutch out: A term, usually with negative connotations, used to indicate to another person that they wish to be left alone or for the other person to leave the area before a fight occurs between them. For example, "I ain't got nothing more to say to you, man, so let your clutch out." Also, see "pop your clutch."

lightbulb: A term used to refer to a life sentence on which the offender becomes eligible for parole in twenty years. For example, "Barry has four lightbulbs." Also, for cross-reference, see "baby life."

like stink on shit: Used to refer to things which match, usually with a negative connotation, or which occur quickly or without question, again with a negative connotation. For example, "Man, did you see Jim go off on Bill? It was like stink on shit." Also, see "like white on rice."

like white on rice: A dated term used to indicate items which are natural, or which go together naturally. Quickly. Without question. For example, "Don got mad at David and was on him like white on rice." Also, see "like stink on shit."

livin' large: Living well. Spending a lot of money in prison. For example, "John is livin' large."

loan shark: Someone who loans money or canteen items to other inmates for a return of interest on the money or items loaned. For example, "Shawn went to the loan shark for some cash." Also referred to as a "shark."

lock-down: A reference to periods of time when the inmate population is confined to the dormitories, usually for security reasons, but sometimes because of weather conditions such as fog, lightening, or dangerous storms. For example, "They had us locked down this morning because of that damn fog."

lock 'n' load: A term referring to preparation to masturbate while watching a female. Prepare to "gun down" a female. For example, "Lock 'n' load, here comes that fine bitch that works in medical."

lock-up: A reference to isolation. To be placed in a prison isolation cell. To be segregated from the rest of the inmate population in prison. For example, "Terry went to lock-up for the last write-up he got." Also, see "hole," "hole time," and "honeycomb hideout."

long lap: A long walk, usually around the perimeter of the yard. For example, "Let's go take a long lap."

Alphabetical Listing

lowdown: 1. Information, facts. To tell the truth or furnish facts about a person or event(s). 2. A dated term used to refer to another individual as being without scruples or untrustworthy. For example, "Here's the lowdown on what happened in the gym this morning." "That Steve is a real lowdown bastard."

Mm

make tracks: To leave. To travel. For example, "I'm ready to make tracks." "We're through talking man, so why don't you just make tracks?"

man: 1. A term used to refer to a correctional officer. For example, "Hey, look out. Here comes the man." 2. A dated term used to refer to any power of authority, usually used by blacks in reference to the white power structure. For example, "The man is always trying to keep a brother down." Also, see "C.O.," "Colonel Klink," and "white shirt."

man down: A term used to indicate that a correctional staff officer or other staff person is approaching. For example, "Hey, you guys, man down."

mash: A dated term used to refer to any homemade wine, usually made with yeast, yeast rolls and dried fruit. For example, "Man, that Rusty can really make some bitchin' mash." Also, see "buck" and "hooch."

max date: The date at which time an inmate is due to be released from prison. A reference to an inmate's maximum release date. For example, "My max date is coming up next year."

max out: A term used to refer to having served all of one's prison sentence. For example, "If Dewey keeps on getting in trouble, he's going to max out his time." Also, see "carry it to the door."

max out camp: A term used to indicate that a particular correctional facility is known, or has a reputation of being a unit where inmates serve most or all of their prison sentence with few or no custody promotions. For example, "Man, this ain't nothing but a max out camp."

may-tag: 1. A term used to refer to an inmate who earns money by washing clothes for other inmates. For example, "Mike earns his hustle as a may-tag." 2. A term used to refer to an inmate who earns money by performing oral sex on other inmates. For example, "That Richard ain't nothing but a may-tag."

Alphabetical Listing

43

meat: A term used to refer to the penis. For example, "He was strokin' his meat and watching that lady at the desk." Also, see "head," and "Johnson."

mojo: A handmade pouch or trinket used to keep or hide money in. For example, "That damn snitch told him where the mojo is."

motel six: A reference to being placed in segregation, or lock-up. Referred to as "motel six" because cells are all single cells, and it is a play on the television advertisements which state "It's cheap and they leave the lights on for you." For example, "Mickey got into some real shit, man, and got himself locked up in motel six." Also, see "hole," "honeycomb hideout," and "lock-up."

mother: A derogatory term used in a variety of ways to denote anything of a negative nature. Also an abbreviation for "mother fucker." For example, "That test was a real mother." "Hey, you mother, I'll bust your damn head."

mother fucker: A derogatory term used in a variety of ways to denote anything of a negative nature. Can be a noun or adjective. For example, "That damn mother fucker stole my canteen." "This camp is a mother fucker." "I had a real mother fucking time of it in county jail."

mother's day: A term referring to the date of receipt of money by an inmate's mother, wife, or

Prison-ese
A Survivor's Guide
To Speaking Prison Slang

girlfriend. Can refer to payday, welfare, disability, Social Security, etc. For example, "My old lady ought to be sending some cash real soon. Next week is mother's day."

mouthpiece: A reference to a person's mouth. For example, "Why don't you just shut your mouthpiece?"

mud duck: A dated term, which refers to an unattractive female. For example, "Bob's girl is just a mud duck."

mule: A dated term, referring to someone or some means of transporting any material, usually drugs. For example, "Greg is a mule."

my mouth ain't bleeding: A challenge to straighten an alleged wrong by fighting. A challenge to a fight. A suggestion to an opponent that he will have to use physical force if he wishes to get revenge or bring about change in the other person's behavior. For example, "I ain't done nothing wrong. My mouth ain't bleeding." Also, see "come get you."

my name's Bennett and I ain't in it: A dated expression to indicate that an inmate will not reveal any information which he may know about another person or incident. For example, "Hey, man, don't ask me. My name's Bennett and I ain't in it."

my word: To be honest. To tell the truth. For example, "I give you my word. I will repay you come Thursday." Also, see "straight up," and "word up."

Nn

nature: A term used to refer to sexual anatomy, physiology, or sexual desire. For example, "Every time I see that bitch, I feel my nature come up on me."

nick: A small amount of marijuana, costing five dollars. For example, "I bought a nick from him yesterday." Also, see "nickel" and "nickel bag."

nickel: 1. A five-dollar bill. 2. A small amount of marijuana, costing five dollars. For example, "He sold me a nickel bag of pot." Also, see "nick," and "nickel bag."

nickel bag: A five-dollar bag of marijuana. For example, "I want a nickel bag, man." Also, see "nick," and "nickel."

Oo

OK Corral: A group of males engaged in gunnin' down a female. A group of males having sexual fantasies while watching a female and masturbating to such fantasies. For example, "The OK Corral formed at the gate when that second shift bitch came in today."

old lady: Wife. Girlfriend. A dated term used to denote a female significant other. For example, "Steve got a visit from his old lady last Sunday."

old man: Husband. Boyfriend. A dated term used to denote a male significant other, but may also refer to one's father. For example, "Jerry's old man don't send him any money."

on like a pot of neckbones: A dated term that refers to fighting. An analogy to a boiling pot of chicken neckbones. For example, "Chris and Brian were getting it on like a pot of neckbones."

Alphabetical Listing

on state: Reference to serving a prison sentence under state law in a state prison. For example, "I been on state since I was 15."

on the fly: While moving. While in transit. For example, "I was in a hurry, so I ate my snack cake on the fly."

on the street: A reference to civilian life. Outside a prison. Prior to incarceration. For example, "I was knockin' down the big bucks out on the street."

overloaded: A term referring to having too much money on one's person. Being in possession of more money than allowed by prison policy. For example, "Don got a write-up for being overloaded."

over the hump: A reference to having served one-half of one's sentence or prison term. For example, "I finish half my time this year. I'm over the hump."

Prison-ese
A Survivor's Guide
To Speaking Prison Slang

Pp

package: A reference to acquired immune deficiency syndrome (AIDS) or the HIV virus. For example, "Bob, I wouldn't be associating with him if I were you. He's got the package." Also, see "slim-fast diet."

pancake: 1. A term used to refer to a bisexual male. One who enjoys sexual contact with both males and females. For example, "Nathan is a pancake." Pancake may also be used to refer to homosexual behavior. 2. This term is used to refer to a person who has a flat butt. For example, "Man, check out that bitch. Ain't nuthin' there but a pancake."

paper: A term used to refer to any amount of paper money. For example, "He has plenty of paper."

park it: To sit. To loiter. To be stationary. To stay in one place. For example, "Hey man, why don't you just park it and chill out for a minute."

partner: Friend. A person with whom one spends a majority of time. For example, "Scott is my partner. I hang with him."

payback: Refers to getting revenge. For example, "He got Bernie, but if I know Bernie, he'll get his payback." Also, see "getback."

Alphabetical Listing

PC: Protective custody. Segregation of inmates from the general population who are under threat or at a risk of physical and/or sexual assault. For example, "Ricky owed so much money he had to go to PC." Also, see "check off," and "honeycomb hideout."

peace up: A dated term used to imply a friendly greeting, usually given with an upside peace sign in which the index finger and middle finger are held in an upside down position next to the heart. For example, "Hey, homie, peace up."

peel your banana: 1. To pull the foreskin of the penis back. For example, "He had to peel his banana when the guard did a shake down." 2. To masturbate. For example, "John's going to peel his banana." Also, see "skin it back."

peel your wig: A reference to fighting. For example, "If you don't get out of my face, I'm going to peel your wig."

penitentiary rich: Having a lot of money by prison standards. Yet, having the same amount outside of prison would not be considered a great deal of money. For example, "He got it going on man. He's penitentiary rich. His old lady sent him in $500 this week!"

phat: (pronounced "fat") A term with a positive connotation, used to describe anyone or anything, which is exceptionally attractive. For example, "She is phat." "His Reeboks are phat."

phone call: A message. To converse. To talk. To indicate that someone wishes to see or talk to another person. For example, "Hey, Walt, you got a phone call on the yard." Typically the phrase is accompanied by a hand signal with the hand to the ear, in a gesture that resembles a telephone. (The thumb is pointed to the ear and the little finger is pointed to the mouth, with the other fingers curled inward.)

pickin': Dated term used to denote interacting with someone playfully. To tease or joke with someone. For example, "Come on, man, he didn't mean no harm. Can't you see he was just pickin'?"

picks: Bets. Placing bets on the score in a sporting event. Picks can be made for scores at the quarter, half-time, game's end, or on each segment of the event. For example, "His picks are 77 and 65 at half-time." Also, see "picks of the week," "play the pool," and "pull the drivers."

pick(s) of the week: Bets for the weeks on sporting events. For example, "My picks of the week are Duke and Carolina."

pissing into the wind: To attempt to achieve a goal which cannot be attained. To be unrealistic, grandiose, or engage in self-defeating behavior.

For example, "If he really thinks he's going to do only five years on a forty-year sentence, he's just pissing into the wind."

pistol: Penis. To prepare to masturbate. To plan to "gun someone down." For example, "That fine lookin' bitch is coming in today. I'm gonna strap on my pistol."

pistol Pete: A reference to someone who masturbates frequently. Also used to refer to someone who guns down females. For example, "That Maurice is a regular pistol Pete." Also, see "gunslinger," "OK Corral," and "shooter."

pitcher: The dominant partner in a male homosexual relationship or act. A reference to the partner in the male homosexual act who inserts his penis into the other partner's mouth or rectum. For example, "Donny and Mike don't swap out. Donny plays pitcher and Mike plays catcher."

play it off: To deny. To discount. To make an excuse. For example, "If the officers ask you anything, just play it off." Also, see "my name's Bennett and I ain't in it."

play the pool: To place a bet or play a parlay ticket on or in some type of sports pool for monetary gain. For example, "Man, that Everett is some kinda lucky. He just won forty bucks by playin' the pool." Also, see "picks," "pick(s) of the week," "playin' the numbers," and "pull the drivers."

**Prison-ese
A Survivor's Guide
To Speaking Prison Slang**

playin' the numbers: A phrase referring to the placing of a bet. Betting. Gambling. Often refers to betting on sporting events. For example, "I won ten bucks last Saturday playin' the numbers." Also, see "picks," "pick(s) of the week," "play the pool," and "pull the drivers."

pluggin': 1. Picking. Teasing. Verbal or physical behavior intended to hurt another person emotionally, mentally, or physically. For example, "Harry was pluggin' Lester about his family." 2. A reference to inserting the penis into someone's vagina or anus. Sexual intercourse. For example, "Tom got caught pluggin' Andy last night in the gym."

police: Correctional officer. For example, "Hey, man, watch out. Here comes the police." Also, see "C.O.," "Colonel Klink," "the man," and "white shirt."

pop your clutch: A dated term now, but still popularly used, usually with negative connotations, to indicate to another person that they wish to be left alone or for the other person to "get lost." For example, "Man can't you take a hint. Pop your clutch." Also, see "let me see the back of your head get small," and "let your clutch out."

pound: A five-dollar bill. For example, "That cat owes me a pound." Also, see "dove," and "nickel."

Alphabetical Listing

53

psych: Psychologist or psychiatrist. For example, "Man, they tell me I got to see the psych and take a test before they'll give me my honor grade." Also, see "bug doctor," "doc," and "shrink."

ptomaine domain: A reference to the inmate cafeteria or "chow hall." For example, "It's lunch time, so I guess we better head on over to ptomaine domain."

pull the drivers: A reference to placing a bet or playing a pool on a race car event. Usually used with regards to NASCAR race season. For example, "Hey, Gordon, you gonna pull the drivers this weekend?"

pull your nuts: To wish someone bad luck, often accompanied by a hand gesture to one's own genitals. For example, "Don't pull your nuts on me. I been at this camp too long and I'm ready to smell some gas."

pump iron: A reference to weight lifting. To lift weights in a competition or to participate in bodybuilding. For example, "That Earl likes to pump iron."

pumping: Masturbation. For example, "I saw David in his bunk pumping away."

punk: A reference to a male homosexual who offers sexual favors for money, drugs, or canteen items. A male prostitute. For example, "Danny ain't

Prison-ese
A Survivor's Guide
To Speaking Prison Slang

nothing but a punk." Also, see "boy," "canteen baby," "pussy boy," and "state baby."

pussy: Dated expression to refer to a female's sexual organs, specifically the vagina. For example, "I'd give a hundred bucks for some pussy."

pussy boy: An inmate who has a reputation for selling sexual favors for money, drugs, canteen items, or protection. For example, "Barry is just a pussy boy." Also, see "boy," "canteen baby," "punk," and "state baby."

put some water on it: A phrase used to request the courtesy that a person using the toilet flush it, in order to reduce the unpleasant odor. For example, "Hey, man, that shit stinks. How about putting some water on it?" Also, see "Why don't you play poker and give it a royal flush?"

put through changes: To aggravate. To surprise. To agitate. To intimidate. To challenge. To present with obstacles. For example, "My woman can't decide whether she wants me any more or not. She just keeps on putting me through changes." Also, see "draggin' me."

Alphabetical Listing

Qq

queen: A reference to a male homosexual who has strongly effeminate mannerisms or behavior. Typically, the most passive partner in a homosexual act or relationship, but not always. For example, "James calls himself 'Silk.' He is some kind of queen!"

Rr

rabbit: A racial slur, referring to a white person. For example, "Hey, man, look at that rabbit."

rabbit blood: To be inclined to run. A high risk for escape. For example, "Tommy has that rabbit blood. He's been busted twice for trying to escape."

rack: Place where one sleeps. Bed. For example, "Hey, man, don't sit on my rack." Also, see "bunk."

rap: 1. Dated term still in wide use that refers to talking or having a conversation. For example, "Yo, homie, let's rap!" 2. Term which implies a particular type of music that is heavily based on rhymes and the street life of gangs. For example, "Dig that video, man. That's a phat rap group, man."

rap dog: A pal. A close friend. Someone you hang with or spend a lot of time with. For example, "Larry is my rap dog." Also, see "partner," and "road dog."

rat: An inmate who has a reputation as an informant. For example, "Hey, man, watch what you tell Eddie. He's a rat." Also, see "snitch."

read my jacket: Implications that there is information on or in an inmate's file which would indicate he is to be feared or given respect for behavior that is dangerous or that he is not one to be messed with. For example, "Before you go shooting off your mouth, you better read my jacket."

ready to roll: A reference to someone who is always prepared, often being extreme or eccentric in their behavior. For example, "That Mickey is always ready to roll." Also, see "wide open."

redneck: A term with negative connotations to some, but held in high regards by others. The following are some of the descriptors or characteristics which are commonly used by prison inmates with reference to the word "redneck." 1. Anyone who holds racist or bigoted attitudes towards non-whites. 2. A farmer or one from a rural area. 3. A person with authority or one who tries to imply he has more authority than he does. 4. Anyone who engages in discriminatory behavior toward another who is of a different race. 5. Someone who is perceived to be a "good ol' boy." 6. A person who is a fan of country western music. 7. Anyone who drives a pickup truck or who drives a truck with a rifle rack in the back window or Confederate flag in the back window. 8. A person of lower education or intelligence. 9. A person who is narrow-minded. 10. A person who has been in the sun too long and has a sunburn on the back of his neck. The possibilities for this term are limitless, and its usage, while dated, is perhaps more popular now because of the comedian Jeff Foxworthy.

reel him in: A prank. To trick someone by devious means, such as lying to them. To trick by bluff or bait someone in order to deceive them. For example, "Did you see how I reeled him in with that bullshit story?"

Prison-ese
A Survivor's Guide
To Speaking Prison Slang

ride: A preference to accompanying someone. Walking with someone. For example, "Mind if I ride along with you to the canteen?"

ride the broom: A spell. A jinx. To wish for something bad to happen to another person. For example, "Don't ride the broom on me."

riding me: Harass. To take advantage of. To pester or bother. For example, "That officer has been riding me ever since I got to this camp." Also, see "doggin' me."

road dog: A pal. A close friend. Someone you spend a lot of time with. This term is more frequently used by white inmates than black inmates, who prefer "rap dog," which means the same thing. For example, "Dennis is my road dog."

rock: 1. One dollar. 2. A reference to cocaine. 3. A dated term used to refer to prison. For example, "Hey, loan me a rock." "Hey, man, my buddy brought in some rock at visitation." "Man, I spent ten years at the rock."

rode hard and put up wet: 1. A reference to one's bad appearance. Appearing as though someone has suffered an ordeal. Disheveled. Ragged. For example, "She looked like she had been rode hard and put up wet today at visitation." 2. To use someone for a favor and then discard them. For example, "He rode hard and put up wet." Also, see "kick to the curb."

roll one: A reference to rolling or making a homemade cigarette. To hand roll a cigarette. May also be used as an invitation for someone to join you in smoking a cigarette. For example, "Hey Jeff, let's go roll one." Also, see "roll-up," and "stud."

roll over: 1. To tell or "snitch" on someone. For example, "Be careful what you say to him. He'll roll over on you." 2. To give up easily. To give in without a fight. For example, "Don't worry about Mickey giving you any trouble. He'll roll over." 3. To budget your money. To make as much profit as possible. To get the most for your money. For example, "I need to roll over all I can to live."

roll-up: A homemade cigarette. A cigarette rolled by hand. For example, "I don't have a Cadillac, but you're welcome to a roll-up." Also, see "roll one," "roll-your-own," and "stud."

roll-your-own: A roll-up. A homemade cigarette. For example, "I got some stud, so go ahead and roll-your-own." Also, see "roll-up," and "stud."

rolled down: To approach or overtake quickly. To take by surprise. To move toward. For example, "The man rolled down on him pretty damn quick."

**Prison-ese
A Survivor's Guide
To Speaking Prison Slang**

run boy: An inmate who runs errands for officers and other staff. A gopher. For example, "The run boy went to the canteen for the officer."

Ss

scarf: To take. To take more than one needs. To do anything quickly. For example, "He can really scarf down his food."

scope out: To observe closely. To observe or look at. For example, "Scope out that female over there. She's nice looking." "The officer was scoping out the dayroom."

screw: 1. To have sexual intercourse. For example, "I damn sure would like to screw that bitch." 2. A dated term, referring to any correctional officer. For example, "Hey, man, look out. Here comes the screw."

scribe: To write. To draft a letter. Any written material. A prolific writer. Someone who has a reputation as a good writer. For example, "John sent a scribe to his mom." "He went to a scribe to get his appeal wrote."

seemore: Correctional officer. Staff person or officer at a prison. For example, "You guys better put a lid on that joint. Here comes seemore." Also, see "C.O.," "police," "screw," "the man," and "white shirt."

sewer trout: Half of a fish; the long variety which are typically served fried in most state prisons. For example, "We're having that fucking sewer trout for supper again tonight."

shadow: 1. A friend. A reference to a person who is usually seen with another. A pal. A partner or sidekick. For example, "Well, there goes Scott with his shadow." 2. To follow another person closely without being seen. To observe another from a distance undetected. For example, "I get the feeling I'm being shadowed."

shakedown: A dated term, but used popularly, to denote being searched by an officer or staff person. Shakedown typically refers to one or more dormitories being systematically searched by prison officials for contraband items, but it can also imply a one-on-one search of an inmate who is suspected of possessing contraband, or is a new arrival at a unit or is returning from a visit. For example, "They had a shakedown in Unit 2 this morning."

Prison-ese
A Survivor's Guide
To Speaking Prison Slang

shank: A homemade weapon, usually fashioned from a piece of metal, tool, or eating utensil stolen from the kitchen or workshop. For example, "I heard he got shookdown and they found a shank under his mattress."

shark: Someone who loans money to others for interest. Also commonly referred to as "loan shark." For example, "Donny went to the shark for some cash to get canteen."

shell: A term used to refer to someone who does not use good judgment. Someone who does not appear to be thinking clearly or be mentally sound. A reference to someone who is not wise, does not have common sense, or is mentally deficient. For example, "He's not wrapped too tight, a real shell." Also, see, "bug," "bug case," and "water head."

ship: To transfer. To move from one location or prison unit to another. For example, "I hear they got a big shipping list for this week." Also, see "ship out," and "smell some gas."

ship out: To be transferred from one prison unit to another. For example, "I've been ready to leave this place, man. I want to ship out." Also, see "ship," and "smell some gas."

shit jacket: Commode or toilet. For example, "Earl was sitting on the shit jacket when they called him to visitation."

shit stirrer: Someone who is known for trying to cause or promote trouble. A troublemaker. For example, "That guy ain't nothin' but a shit stirrer."

shoe leather: Roast beef that is served by the state, commonly known to be tough and stringy. For example, "Well, it's Sunday. I guess that means shoe leather for lunch."

shooter: A reference to someone who is a frequent masturbator. An inmate who "guns down" female staff. For example, "That Maurice is a shooter." Also, see, "gun slinger," "OK Corral," and "pistol Pete."

shootin' boosters: To boost. To encourage someone to do something daring. A person known to cause trouble or promote same. For example, "Jack is shootin' boosters to Brian."

short: A portion of a cigarette. For example, "Say, can you save me a short?"

short lap: A short walk, usually around the prison unit compound or track. For example, "Let's take a short lap."

short me out: To request or to save a part of a cigarette for someone. For example, "Yo, homie, short me out on that Kool."

shrink: A term, although dated, used to refer to any mental health profession. For example, "Benny went to see the shrink." Also, see, "bug doctor," "head doctor," and "psych."

sidekick: Friend. Pal. Partner. A dated term but still used widely. For example, "Jim is a sidekick to Bert."

signify: Profiling. Showing off. To engage in impression management. A reference to any behavior performed for attention or an effect. Any attempt to impress or gain the attention of others through outrageous or outlandish methods of behavior. For example, "Terry put up his fists, but he won't fight. He's just signifying."

skeet: To ejaculate. Discharge of semen from the penis. For example, "Doc, I can't skeet when I take that medication."

skeezer: A female who has an unattractive face but usually an attractive body. For example, "I saw his girlfriend last week at visitation and she's a real skeezer." Also, see "dog," and "mud duck."

skin: A reference to beating someone. To win. For example, "I can skin him at horseshoes."

skin it back: 1. To pull the foreskin of the penis back. For example, "During shakedown, the guard told him to skin it back." 2. To masturbate. For example, "I heard they caught John at school trying to skin it back." Also, see "gun down," and "peel your banana."

skint: To have beaten someone or to have been beaten, usually at a game of cards or horseshoes, but can also apply to being the victim of a con game or the perpetrator of a con game. For example, "I skint him at spades twice today." Also, see "skin."

skull and brains: Giving or receiving oral sex. For example, "I'm going to get some skull and brains."

sky: To jump. To jump high. To jump well. Usually in reference to playing basketball. For example, "He's pretty good in basketball. He can really sky."

slim-fast diet: A reference to someone who is suspected of having or has in fact acquired immune deficiency syndrome (AIDS) or the HIV virus. For example, "Bob, I would be careful if I was you. That guy is on the slim-fast diet."

slippin' and slidin': Being evasive. Avoiding the point. Beating around the bush. For example, "I tried to get Jim to give me an answer, but he kept slippin' and slidin'."

smell some gas: To travel by motor vehicle. Usually applied to inmates being transferred. For example, "Man, I'm ready to smell some gas and get the hell away from this place." Also, see "ship," and "ship out."

Prison-ese
A Survivor's Guide
To Speaking Prison Slang

snitch: A dated term, but used commonly, to denote an inmate who has a reputation as an informant to the officers or prison administration. For example, "Hey, don't tell that guy a thing. He's a snitch." Also, see "rat" and "tell."

spike a point: A homemade syringe. To use a homemade syringe. For example, "Rusty is gone to spike a point."

spittin' game: Trying to trick or deceive another person. Trying to fool someone to see if they can be deceived. For example, "I was putting the spittin' game down on Thomas this morning."

split your wig: To fight. To make a threat of violence towards another person. For example, "Man, I done told you to burn the road up before I split your wig."

spray: 1. Flatulence. To pass gas. To "fart." For example, "Yo, man, don't spray around here. Go outside or someplace to do that." 2. To ejaculate while masturbating. For example, "Some guy sprayed all over the damn shower."

spread your cheeks: To separate the buttocks with both hands, usually during a body search or strip search shakedown by a correctional officer. Given to an inmate as an order or command by the officer conducting the search. For example, "Okay, drop 'em and spread your cheeks."

square: A cigarette. For example, "Hey, dude, could you spare a square?"

squirrel: To horde or hide something, usually canteen items or contraband. For example, "I heard they busted Webster for squirreling away over a case of candy bars."

stag: A short of a cigarette. For example, "Hey, man, can you spare a stag?" Also, see "short," and "short me out."

state baby: A reference to an inmate who is the weaker or passive partner in a homosexual relationship, or who submits to a stronger, more dominant partner, or who relies on another inmate for support or protection. For example, "That Tony is just a state baby." Also, see "canteen baby."

state daddy: A reference to an inmate who is the dominate partner in a homosexual relationship, or who takes care of and/or protects the weaker, passive partner. For example, "Jim is Don's state daddy." Also, see "daddy," "state baby," and "sugar daddy."

stim-fast diet: A reference to someone who is addicted to crack cocaine, and has lost an excessive amount of weight. For example, "I hear that Tommy was on that stim-fast diet out on the streets."

**Prison-ese
A Survivor's Guide
To Speaking Prison Slang**

storebox: Canteen. Inmate commissary. One or more locations within a prison unit where inmates may purchase food, cosmetics and assorted sundries. For example, "I'm going to the storebox. Want anything?"

stove: To hit someone. For example, "He felt that the dude did him wrong, so he stove his face in."

straight: A term used to refer to a person who avoids trouble, or does not engage in any type of illegal behavior, in prison or on the street. Someone who is honest and/or trustworthy. Straightforward. For example, "You can trust Gene. He's straight."

straight up: 1. A truthful statement. Used when someone wishes to convey honesty and sincerity. For example, "Straight up. I saw the dude steal your radio, man." Also, see "my word," and "word up."

straighten: To correct or make right some wrongdoing or perceived injustice. To exact revenge or repayment for being treated unfairly or taken advantage of. For example, "He felt he had to straighten it."

strapped: To have something, usually a large amount of money or a weapon, or even drugs. For example, "From the looks of his locker, he was strapped with cosmetics." "Bill was strapped

Alphabetical Listing

with a shank when the C.O. stopped him and did a search."

strapped down: A term used synonymously with "strapped." For example, "I heard they caught Charles strapped down with pot."

street: A reference to civilian life. Outside of prison. Prior to being incarcerated. For example, "I was really knockin' down the big bucks on the street."

string: A method of sending messages by string, usually by hanging the message out a window or flushing the message or object down a toilet, attached to a string, and then recovered by a recipient at another location. For example, "I got word on the shakedown by string." Also, see "kite flush."

strip search: The search of a prison inmate, during which the inmate is required to remove all his or her clothing. For example, "Man, the only thing I hate about visits is the damn strip search." Also, see "shakedown," and "spread your cheeks."

strong-arm: To take something from someone by physical force or threat of physical force. Robbery by physical force. For example, "Don't try to strong-arm me, man. I been down too long for that shit."

stud: The loose tobacco sold in inmate canteens which has to be hand-rolled. For example, "They

Prison-ese
A Survivor's Guide
To Speaking Prison Slang

went up on stud in the canteen to forty cents a pack." Also, see "roll-up."

sucker: Fool. Someone who is easily tricked. Someone who is gullible. For example, "I got over on him cause he's a real sucker."

sugar daddy: An older man who pays his sexual partners. A reference to the partner in a relationship who provides monetary or material rewards to the other partner in return for sex. A reference to a male partner in a relationship who is used as a source of support. For example, "All he is, is a sugar daddy to him/her." Also, see "canteen baby," and "state daddy."

suitcase: To insert something into the rectum, usually for the purpose of concealing or hiding contraband, i.e., drugs, money, or a weapon. For example, "I heard that Dave got in some pot at visit by suitcasing it." Suitcasing is usually accomplished by wrapping the item in clear plastic wrap, tin foil, or in a balloon.

swap out: To take turns in homosexual activity. Usually refers to one partner inserting his penis into the other partner's mouth or rectum, then allowing the other partner to do the same. For example, "They caught Mickey and Tom in the bathroom last night swapping out." Also, see "AC/DC," "catcher," and "pitcher."

sweat: 1. A term referring to watching something or someone with intensity. To stare with a glare or leer. To watch or observe closely or carefully. For example, "Hey, man, what you sweatin' me for?" 2. To worry. For example, "Don't sweat that write-up dude. They'll probably dismiss it."

sweatin': A term used synonymously with sweat, to refer to watching someone or something with close intensity. For example, "The man was sweatin' us last night." Also, see "hawk."

sweet: A term referring to being gay. A homosexual. For example, "I think that guy is a little sweet." Also, see "He's got sugar in his blood."

switch hitter: 1. Someone who masturbates with both hands, left then right. For example, "He's a real switch hitter with that dong." 2. Someone who has sex with both males and females. For example, "I heard that Will is a switch hitter."

Tt

take care of business: A reference to almost any activity. For example, to masturbate; to "straighten" something or to settle debts; to do or finish a job; to collect money owed or to seek revenge on someone; to exact justice or put things right either for a real or perceived wrong. For example, "Frank is takin' care of business."

taking off a piece of work: A phrase referring to masturbation. For example, "John is taking off a piece of work."

talk game: A reference to someone who speaks authoritatively and readily. A fast or smooth talker. Speaking in a convincing manner. For example, "That Mike has a good talk game."

tell: A reference to informing on another inmate. For example, "Don't do anything around Eric. He'll tell." Also, see "rat" and "snitch."

the bitch: A reference to the habitual felon act or sentence. The term of a sentence imposed as a result of the habitual felony charge and conviction. For example, "I got the bitch for the last crime I done."

the man: A term, although dated, still widely used in reference to a correctional officer or any staff person in a correctional facility or anyone in an authority position. For example, "Man, you better watch out. Here comes the man."

the wall: A reference to a maximum security prison. In North Carolina, "the wall" refers to Central Prison in Raleigh. For example, "I spent the last seven years at the wall."

thick: A street phrase widely used in prison, with positive connotation, referring to a female's thighs. For example, "The bitch with the red dress on is thick."

three for five: The interest that a loan shark will charge for loaned money or canteen items. Three (dollars or items) are loaned out with the agreement that five will be paid back. Also, the rates will vary, and can be "two for three," "one for two," and even "two for five."

throw hands: To prepare for a fight. To fight. For example, "They were going to throw hands over the canteen line."

throw some groceries down my neck: To eat. For example, "I'm going to the canteen to throw some groceries down my neck."

ticket: 1. A piece of paper on which an inmate has written his bid or bet on any type of wager or pool. Picks in a sporting event. Can also be a verbal wager or bet. For example, "I hit on the game today, so I'm gonna cash in my ticket after chow call." 2. **To be ticketed, or "written-up."** To receive an infraction or disciplinary write up or charge. A written document delivered to an inmate who has violated prison rules or policy. The initial step in the disciplinary process in a prison. For example, "Officer Byrd gave him a ticket for having over thirty bucks in his locker." 3. A document or piece of paper indicating that an inmate has a visit or visitors. For example, "Yo, man, the C.O. just came in with a ticket. You got somebody at visitation."

ticket man: The person responsible for collecting, holding and paying off tickets in a gambling pool. The ticket man pays off the "picks of the week" on bets on a sporting event. For example, "Hey, ticket man, pay up. I hit on the pool."

time stretcher: An inmate who usually has a short period of time or a brief sentence and typically has an attitude problem, provoking fights with inmates serving a longer sentence. For example, "That damn kid in B dorm ain't nothin' but a time stretcher, man. Don't even get in with him."

to death: A dated term, referring to anything exceptionally good or desirable. For example, "That new bitch on second shift is thick to death."

to die for: A dated term with reference to anything that is especially desirable or in short supply in a prison. For example, "Man, I'd give anything for a beer! A cold one is to die for!"

Alphabetical Listing

75

trap off: To trick or deceive. To frame. A reference to entrapment. To set up. For example, "I didn't do anything, man. They just trying to trap me off!"

tree-jumper: A term used to refer to an inmate who is serving, or is believed to be serving a sentence for a sex offense, particularly rape. For example, "Hey, Bob, I hear your homeboy is a tree jumper."

trey-piece: A reference to three of anything. Often used to refer to three punches in a fist fight or three of a kind in a game of cards. For example, "John hit Bill with a trey-piece." "I was playing spades last night and got hit with a damn trey-piece."

trim: Sexual intercourse. A term used to refer to a woman's vagina. A female's sexual organs. For example, "When I get out of here, the first thing I'm gonna do is find me some trim." Also, see "cock" and "pussy."

try: To test. To provoke or attempt to intimidate. To test one's limits or boundaries. For example, "I done told you, man, not to try me. I'll bust your grill."

turn him out: A reference to raping someone or otherwise engaging in anal intercourse with another inmate for the first time, usually by force or by threat of force, intimidation or coercion. For example, "I hear Rick plans to turn out ol' Bobby tonight."

Prison-ese
A Survivor's Guide
To Speaking Prison Slang

turn key: A reference to a correctional officer. For example, "Hey, turn key! They made school call. Open this damn gate!" Also, see "C.O.," "Colonel Klink," "the man," and "white shirt."

turn over: To budget your money or make a wise investment with it. To get the most for your money. For example, "Man, I got to turn over at least ten bucks a week to get by." Also, see "roll over."

turned out: A reference to an inmate who has been raped or anally penetrated for the first time. Usually by force, threat of force, or by means of intimidation or coercion. For example, "I hear Richard was turned out in the county jail."

twenty-four/seven (24/7): Twenty-four hours a day, seven days a week. All the time. For example, "Man, working in that mother fucking kitchen is 24/7."

twist: To hand-roll a cigarette. To make a cigarette. An invitation to have someone join you in making and smoking hand-rolled cigarettes. For example, "Hey, Bill, let's twist."

two-piece: A reference to two of anything. Often used to refer to punches in a fist fight. For example, "I hear that Eddie put a two-piece on Jeff's grill."

two-time loser: Someone who is a recidivist and is serving time in prison for the second time. For example, "Man, that David is a two-time loser."

Uu

under the gun: A reference to being at a prison unit which has guard towers manned by officers who are armed. For example, "I was under the gun for five years."

Vv

V: A visit, For example, "I'm expecting a "V" on Sunday."

Ww

wad: A large sum of money. A large roll of paper money. For example, "Did you see that wad that C.O. took out of his pocket?"

wannabe: An impersonator. One who is a fake or pretender. A false front or façade. A term used to describe an inmate who affiliates with a particular social or ethnic group and imitates the behavior and/or language of the group. It's usually obvious that the person is putting up a false front and doesn't belong to the group. For example, "That Jack ain't no bad ass. He's just a wannabe."

waterhead: A term referring to someone who uses poor judgment or who is a slow learner or has mental retardation. Mental deficiency. Someone who exhibits bizarre behavior. An idiot. Stupid. Someone who exhibits behavior inappropriate to the situation. Someone to be avoided or ignored. For example, "He's a waterhead, man, a real wacko."

Alphabetical Listing

79

what do you know: A request for information. A salutation or general greeting synonymous with "Hello, how are you?" For example, "Yo, dude, what do you know?"

what goes around, comes around: The way you treat someone is the way you will be treated. "An eye for an eye and a tooth for a tooth." Sometimes issued as a threat, suggesting the person will suffer consequences as a result of their actions. For example, "You might think you're getting over on me, but just remember, what goes around, comes around."

what's going on: A general greeting. A request for information or the latest gossip. Also said as "what's *really* going on?" to imply that something perverse or devious is happening. For example, "So, hey, man, what's going on?" "Wait a minute. What's really going on?"

what's hangin': A general greeting. A request for information. Synonymous with "what's happening?" and "what's going on?" For example, "Hey, homie, what's hangin'?"

what's happening: A general greeting. A request for information. Rather dated, but still in wide use in most prisons. For example, "Hey, man, what's happening?"

what's shakin': A general greeting. A term synonymous with "what's going on?," "what's hangin'?," "what's happening?" For example, "Yo, dude, what's shakin'?"

what's up: Popular greeting, made so by the television show *Martin*. Term is synonymous with "what's hangin'?," "what's happening?," and "what's shakin'?" For example, "Hey, man, what's up?"

whine: To complain. To indulge in self-pity. To feel sorry for one's self. For example, "Hey, man, shut yer whining. Leave something for the baby to do!" Also, see "bitch."

white shirt: A correctional officer above the rank of sergeant. A captain or lieutenant. For example, "Look out, man, a white shirt just walked in." Also, see "Colonel Klink."

who owns the lowball: A request to know what inmate owns the lowball card game in or on a particular dorm, housing unit, or yard. Most games are owned by an inmate who receives a percentage from the participants, in a prison version of a business franchise. For example, "So tell me, who owns the low ball?" Can also be said as, "Who owns the pool?" "Who owns the five card (or seven card)?"

why don't you play poker and give it a royal flush: A request for someone to flush the toilet. For example, "Hey, man, how about playing poker and give it a royal flush? That shit stinks!" Also, see "put some water on it."

wide open: A reference to a state or trait, suggesting the person has no limits or any boundaries. Failure to set limits on one's own behavior. Bizarre behavior. Impulsiveness. Poor judgment. For example, "Ken will say just about anything. He's wide open."

woofin': Bluffing. To make an idle threat. For example, "You ain't gonna do nuthin' but stand there woofin'." Also, see "woof tickets."

woof tickets: To make idle threats or bluff with no intention of carrying out or making good the threats. For example, "Are you gonna do something about it or just stand there selling woof tickets?"

word up: A truthful statement. Used when someone wishes to convey honesty or imply sincerity in a statement. Honest. For example, "Hey, man, word up. I saw it myself."

working out: Masturbating. For example, "Phil is in the toilet again working out."

write-up: To be given a disciplinary infraction or charge. To be "ticketed." A violation of rules or policy in the D.O.C. For example, "Rusty got a write-up for going through the chow line twice at lunch."

Prison-ese
A Survivor's Guide
To Speaking Prison Slang

yard: Any area within a prison facility or compound, outside a dormitory or other building. For example, "Let's go out on the yard and take a lap."

yard closed: A reference to periods of time when the inmate population is confined to the dormitories or units, usually for security reasons. For example, "Hey, they just called yard closed."

yard queer: A derogatory term used to refer to homosexuals. Someone who sells sexual favors for money, drugs, and/or canteen. For example, "I hear that Jim is a yard queer." Also, see "boy," "canteen baby," and "state baby."

you ain't gonna bust a grape: A phrase often issued as a challenge for someone to take some action. A dare or bluff. To call someone's bluff. An insult directed toward another inmate's integrity or ability to fight. For example, "You ain't gonna do a damn thing! You wouldn't bust a grape."

you know what's going on: A term synonymous with "you know what's happening." For example, "Yeah, it's me. You know what's going on. It's payday and you owe me five bucks. Pay up!"

you know what's happening: A suggestion that another party should be informed. They should know what is going on or what is happening. A phrase used to indicate that it is time for some event to occur or take place, such as when payment on a debt is due. For example, "You know what's happening. It's payday!"

you know what time it is: A phrase synonymous with "you know what's happening," and/or "you know what's going on." Implies that the other person should have knowledge of what is happening or what is about to occur. For example, "That's right, it's me. You know what time it is! Payday!"

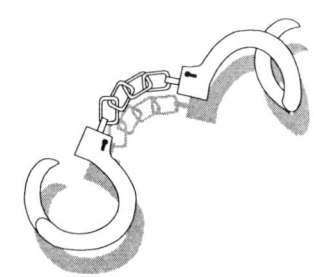

About the Author

Gary K. Farlow attended Guilford Technical Community College, majoring in Administration of Justice. He completed undergraduate studies at the John Marshall School of Law in Atlanta, and earned a Juris Doctorate from the Thomas Jefferson College of Law at Heed University in Christianstead, St. Croix, U.S. Virgin Islands. He is past chairman of the Greensboro Human Relations Commission; represented former North Carolina Governor James G. Martin on the North Carolina Board of Examiners for Nursing Home Administrators; represented North Carolina at the 1984 National Conference on the Aged; was Reagan and Bush Administration nominee for the African Development Foundation; served on the United Arts Council of Greensboro, The Community Theatre of Greensboro, the Young Artists Opera Theatre and Guild, the Easter Music Festival, the English Speaking Union of the Triad, the Greensboro Historical Museum and Society, the Greensboro Area Chamber of Commerce. He is a former vice president of the Gate City Jaycees, a Lion, and founder of the Senior Theatre Consortium. Mr. Farlow's previous writings have appeared in *Chicken*

Soup for the Prisoner's Soul, the *Journal of the American Health Care Association*, two poetic anthologies of the National Library of Poetry, *Essence of a Dream* and *Visions*, and *Pathways*, published by the Anson County Writers Club. He is a former Associate Editor of *The East Triad Press* and *The Greensboro Sun*, Sports Reporter for *The High Point Enterprise*, and has done various features for the *Greensboro News and Record*. Additionally, Mr. Farlow has written a playscript entitled *Sticks*, which deals with the HIV/AIDS epidemic in the nation's prison system. His works are contained in three poetry chapbooks, *Conferring With the Moon*, *After Midnight* and *Into the Abyss*, all his own works. His poetry has been released on audiocassette by the National Library of Poetry and is entitled *Visions*. Mr. Farlow has traveled extensively and has been a guest lecturer at Rand Afrikaans University in Johannesburg, South Africa and at the Medical University of South Africa in Pretoria. His poetry has recently been released in two additional anthologies, *Collections*, by the Illiad Press, and *The Best Poetry of America*, by the National Library of Poetry. Mr. Farlow is single and is an ordained minister with the United Christian Church.

YOU WILL ALSO WANT TO READ:

☐ **76059 HOW TO CLEAR YOUR ADULT AND JUVENILE CRIMINAL RECORDS,** *by William Rinehart.* Author William Rinehart is well-qualified to dispense advice on how to clear one's criminal records. He had two felony convictions and over 30 misdemeanors to his credit before he took the necessary steps to cleanse his adult and juvenile records. Now Rinehart's criminal records are purged of serious offenses, and he shares his hard-earned secrets in this unique sourcebook, which contains never-before revealed step-by-step instructions, along with example forms and comprehensive state-by-state lists of the statutes and laws which must be cited. *1997, 5½ x 8½, 112 pp, illustrated, soft cover. $12.95.*

☐ **76041 THE OUTLAW'S BIBLE, How to Evade the System Using Constitutional Strategy,** *by E.X. Boozhie.* The best "jailhouse" law book ever published — for people on the outside who want to stay there. This is a real life civics lesson for citizen lawbreakers: how to dance on the fine line between freedom and incarceration, how to tiptoe the tightrope of due process. Covers detention, interrogation, searches and seizures. The Constitution is the only non-violent weapon available for those on the wrong side of the law; this book tells you how to wield it. *1985, 5½ x 8½, 336 pp, indexed, soft cover. $16.95.*

☐ **40083 YOU ARE GOING TO PRISON,** *by Jim Hogshire.* This is the most accurate, no-bullshit guide to prison life we have ever seen. Topics covered include: custody; prison; jailhouse justice; execution and much more. When are public defenders your best option? What was Mike Tyson's second biggest mistake? How do you stay on the good side of the guards and other prisoners? If you or a loved one is about to be swallowed up by the system, you need this information if you hope to come out whole. *1994, 5½ x 8½, 185 pp, indexed, soft cover. $14.95.*

☐ **58100 HOW TO SURVIVE FEDERAL PRISON CAMP, A Guidebook for Those Caught Up in the System,** *by Clive Sharp with an Introduction by Claire Wolfe.* Author Clive Sharp, a graduate of the American federal prison camp system, has compiled an essential guidebook that is designed to make a prison camp resident's life bearable. Sharp provides tips that range from presentencing considerations and making prior arrangements; medical and dental advice; realities from day-to-day existence; various camp regulations; work assignments; on through how to deal with halfway houses, supervised release, and getting a post-camp job and restoring civil rights. Absolutely essential reading for anyone who is going to do time in a federal prison camp. *1997, 5½ x 8½, 170 pp, illustrated, soft cover. $16.95.*

☐ **40071 THE BIG HOUSE, How American Prisons Work,** *by Tony Lesce.* This is not a collection of reform theories. Rather, this book is a thorough examination of how prisons work: How do you house, feed, and control thousands of violent, angry people? It examines the prison system from all sides: the inmates, the guards, the politicians, the taxpayers. And it takes a gritty look at issues like capital punishment, psychosurgery, riot control and dealing with the sexual needs of prisoners. The author understands the interplay between convicts and their keepers. After reading this, you will too. *1991, 8½ x 11, 188 pp, illustrated, indexed, soft cover. $19.95.*

☐ **40070 SURVIVING IN PRISON,** *by Harold S. Long.* Convicts don't live in prisons, they survive them. A disturbing account of life behind bars. The author has spent the last ten years in prison. He describes how prisons are run: the penal code and the cellblock code. He takes you out to the yard and into the hole. He explains why rehabilitation programs fail. He discusses isolation units, power structures, and litigation. And he reveals what is required to survive the personal degradation, brutality and humiliation found in contemporary American prisons. *1990, 8½ x 11, 128 pp, soft cover. $14.95.*

Please send me the books I have marked below:

- ☐ 76059 How to Clear Your Adult and Juvenile Criminal Records, $12.95
- ☐ 76041 The Outlaw's Bible, $16.95
- ☐ 40083 You Are Going to Prison, $14.95
- ☐ 58100 How to Survive Federal Prison Camp, $16.95
- ☐ 40071 The Big House, $19.95
- ☐ 40070 Surviving in Prison, $14.95
- ☐ 88888 2002 Loompanics Unlimited Main Catalog, $5.00, see the catalog ad on the next page.

PE2

LOOMPANICS UNLIMITED
PO BOX 1197
PORT TOWNSEND, WA 98368

Please send me the books I have checked above. I am enclosing $ _____ which includes $5.95 for shipping and handling of orders up to $25.00. Add $1.00 for each additional $25.00 ordered. *Washington residents please include 8.2% for sales tax.*

NAME _____

ADDRESS _____

CITY _____

STATE/ZIP _____

We accept Visa, Discover, and MasterCard.
To place a credit card order *only,*
call 1-800-380-2230, 24 hours a day, 7 days a week
or fax us your order at 1-360-385-7785.
Check out our Web site:
www.loompanics.com

The Best Book Catalog In The World!!

We offer hard-to-find books on the world's most unusual subjects. Here are a few of the topics covered IN DEPTH in our exciting new catalog:

Hiding/Concealment of physical objects! A complete section of the best books ever written on hiding things.
Fake ID/Alternate Identities! The most comprehensive selection of books on this little-known subject ever offered for sale! You have to see it to believe it!
Investigative/Undercover methods and techniques! Professional secrets known only to a few, now revealed to you to use! Actual police manuals on shadowing and surveillance!
And much, much, more, including Locks and Lock Picking, Self-Defense, Intelligence Increase, Life Extension, Money-Making Opportunities, Human Oddities, Exotic Weapons, Sex, Drugs, Anarchism, and more!

Our book catalog is over 250 pages, 8½ x 11, packed with more than 800 of the most controversial and unusual books ever printed! You can order every book listed! Periodic supplements keep you posted on the LATEST titles available!!! Our catalog is **$5.00**, including shipping and handling.

Our book catalog is truly THE BEST BOOK CATALOG IN THE WORLD! Order yours today. You will be very pleased, we know.

**LOOMPANICS UNLIMITED
PO BOX 1197
PORT TOWNSEND, WA 98368**

Name _____
Address _____
City/State/Zip _____

We accept Visa, Discover, and MasterCard. For credit card orders *only,* call 1-800-380-2230, 24 hours a day, 7 days a week.
Check out our Web site: www.loompanics.com